PAPERFILMS

ADAPTIVE
COMICS

Written by
JIMMY PALMIOTTI & JUSTIN GRAY

Artwork by
JAVIER PINA

Colors by
ALESSIA NOCERA

Lettering by
BILL TORTOLINI

Cover by
AMANDA CONNER & PAUL MOUNTS

Special addition cover by
DAVE JOHNSON

Design by
JOHN J. HILL

Edited by
JOANNE STARER

Project Manager
PATRICK WEDGE

Co-published by
PAPERFILMS & ADAPTIVE STUDIOS
paperfilms.com
adaptivestudios.com

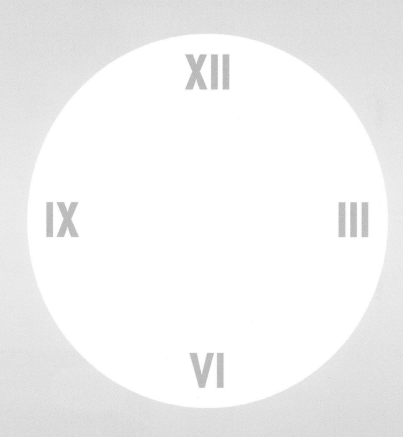

MISS MARR, MY NAME IS EMILY REDGRAVE. DO YOU KNOW WHY YOU'RE HERE?

I'M NOT INTERESTED.

I'M NOT INTERESTED IN WHATEVER *THIS* IS.

EXCUSE ME?

WHAT DO YOU *THINK* THIS IS?

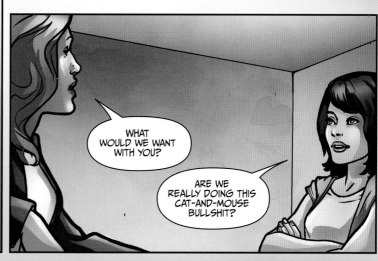

I WANT TO SAY YOU'RE *CIA*, BUT THE LEVEL OF CONFIDENCE YOU'RE EXUDING MAKES ME THINK YOU'RE *DOD* OR HOMELAND.

WHAT WOULD WE WANT WITH YOU?

ARE WE REALLY DOING THIS CAT-AND-MOUSE BULLSHIT?

FINE.

IT IS OBVIOUS YOU'RE PART OF SOME MILITARY SCIENCE DIVISION AND YOU'VE GOT A PROBLEM YOU THINK I CAN FIX.

I'M STILL NOT INTERESTED.

YOUR LECTURE WAS VERY INFORMATIVE...

REGARDLESS OF ADVANCES IN SCIENCE AND TECHNOLOGY, WE CANNOT SURRENDER OUR HUMANITY TO RADICAL ENHANCEMENT, *ESPECIALLY* WHERE OUR SOLDIERS ARE CONCERNED.

I'M NOT SAYING THE DEFINITION OF *HUMAN* WON'T CHANGE. IT MOST CERTAINLY WILL AS WE BREAK THE BONDS OF BIOLOGY. BUT WE MUST RETAIN OUR COMPASSION AND CAPACITY FOR LOVE.

TEO

THAT'S RIDICULOUS! IT'LL NEVER HAPPEN.

INSTEAD YOU'L HAVE THE WEALTHY ELITE CREATING AN ENTIRELY NEW SUBCLASS OF HUMANS OUT OF PEOPLE WHO CAN'T AFFORD EQUALITY IN GENETICS.

HISTORICALLY THAT HAPPENS WITH EVERY EMERGENT TECHNOLOGY.

AND THE FURTHER WE REMOVE OURSELVES FROM OUR HUMANITY, THE MORE LIKELY THAT IS TO HAPPEN. WE HAVE TO RETAIN OUR COMPASSION FOR OTHERS, OUR ABILITY TO EMPATHIZE.

EARLIER YOU MENTIONED THE ABILITY FOR PEOPLE TO TURN OFF THOSE VERY EMOTIONS THAT ARE ESSENTIAL TO YOUR ARGUMENT.

I'M AN OPTIMIST. I BELIEVE CERTAIN HIGH-PRESSURE OR EXTREMELY DANGEROUS PROFESSIONS WILL BENEFIT FROM LIMITED EMOTIONAL SUPPRESSION.

LIKE SOLDIERS ON THE BATTLEFIELD.

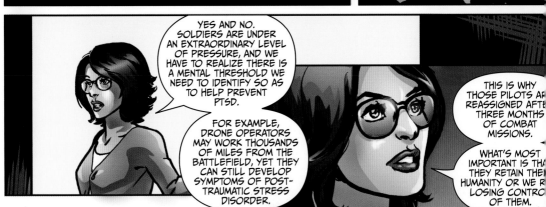

YES AND NO. SOLDIERS ARE UNDER AN EXTRAORDINARY LEVEL OF PRESSURE, AND WE HAVE TO REALIZE THERE IS A MENTAL THRESHOLD WE NEED TO IDENTIFY SO AS TO HELP PREVENT PTSD.

FOR EXAMPLE, DRONE OPERATORS MAY WORK THOUSANDS OF MILES FROM THE BATTLEFIELD, YET THEY CAN STILL DEVELOP SYMPTOMS OF POST-TRAUMATIC STRESS DISORDER.

THIS IS WHY THOSE PILOTS AR REASSIGNED AFTE THREE MONTHS OF COMBAT MISSIONS.

WHAT'S MOST IMPORTANT IS THA THEY RETAIN THE HUMANITY OR WE R LOSING CONTRO OF THEM.

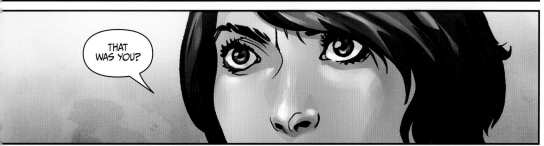

PARK

NO IDEA.

KILLIAN?

CHECKING MY READINGS.

WHO ARE YOU, AND WHAT THE FUCK IS THIS?

THIS IS SOME *DARPA* BULLSHIT, ISN'T IT?

GENTLEMEN, GO FIND SOMETHING TO HIDE BEHIND.

HE'S LIVE. ALL PROGRAMS ARE ACTIVATED.

REPEAT THE MISSION PARAMETERS.

RESCUE HOSTAGES. NEUTRALIZE THE THREAT, AND CAPTURE MARCUS WILLIAM WRIGHT. ALIVE.

THUNK

WELCOME, FRIEND.

KRAK

YOU ARE UNDER ARREST.

I'M NOT. THE LAWS OF MAN CANNOT RESTRAIN ME. YOU CANNOT HAVE THE CHILDREN.

THEY'RE AMONG TH ANGELS.

FWWOOOSSH

YOUR BLOOD-STAINED HANDS CANNOT REACH THEM.

DAMMIT! WHY DIDN'T HE STOP HIM?

HE JUS STOOD TH AND DI NOTHIN

GOOD LORD...

YES. IT'S A LOT TO ABSORB AT FIRST.

HE'S...

IT'S THE ONLY WAY TO MAINTAIN HIM. WE'VE MANAGED TO CREATE A WINDOW OF FORTY-FIVE MINUTES WHERE HE CAN BE FULLY OPERATIONAL, BUT BEYOND THAT, HIS METABOLISM...

I MEAN, *DAMN*...WHAT ARE YOU FEEDING HIM?

WE DON'T. THE BIOWARE KEEPS HIM IN PEAK PHYSICAL CONDITION BECAUSE THE VAST MAJORITY OF HIS TIME IS SPENT IN CRYOSTASIS.

HONESTLY, MISS MARR, YOU ACT LIKE YOU'VE NEVER SEEN A GROWN MAN PRACTICALLY NAKED.

I'VE BEEN SINGLE... FOR...*A WHILE.*

WHAT DO YOU MEAN HE'S ONLY OPERATIONAL FOR FORTY-FIVE MINUTES?

THE TECHNOLOGY THAT MAKES HIM SPECIAL CAN ALSO KILL HIM.

THE FIRST TEST SUBJECTS BURNED OUT IN LESS THAN THIRTY MINUTES. IT HAS TAKEN A BILLION DOLLARS TO ADD THOSE ADDITIONAL FIFTEEN MINUTES.

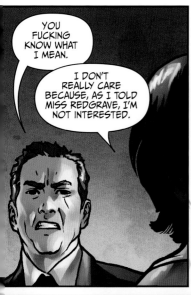

YOU FUCKING KNOW WHAT I MEAN.

I DON'T REALLY CARE BECAUSE, AS I TOLD MISS REDGRAVE, I'M NOT INTERESTED.

YOU DIDN'T TELL HER, DID YOU?

I WAS HOPING TO AVOID IT.

AVOID WHAT?

YOU DON'T HAVE A CHOICE.

YOU'RE NOT GOING TO PULL THAT "I'VE SEEN TOO MUCH" BULLSHIT, ARE YOU?

YOU HAVE TO TAKE THE JOB, AMANDA.

OR WHAT?

OR YOU GET TO SHARE A BUNK BED WITH EDDIE SNOWDEN IN PUTIN'S HOUSE.

DO YOU LISTEN TO YOURSELF? YOU SOUND LIKE AN ASSHOLE.

MR. PARKER IS PRONE TO CARICATURE, BUT THAT DOESN'T CHANGE THE FACT THAT YOU'RE EITHER ON THE TEAM OR YOU'RE SOMEPLACE YOU REALLY DON'T WANT TO BE.

FUCK YOU. BOTH OF YOU.

GOOD LUCK OUT THERE WITH NO MONEY, NO CREDIT, NO PLACE TO LIVE, AND NO WAY OF EARNING A LIVING. YOU WON'T EVEN HAVE A SOCIAL SECURITY NUMBER AN HOUR FROM NOW.

WHY?

FREEDOM AND DEMOCRACY ARE AN ILLUSION. SACRIFICES NEED TO BE MADE FOR THE GREATER GOOD.

OR BAD LUCK ON YOUR PART? PICK ONE.

I HAVE LUNCH WITH SENATOR FAIRBANKS IN HALF AN HOUR. CAN WE WRAP THIS UP?

MAKE HIM GO AWAY.

I WISH I COULD.

WHAT CHANGED? THERE'S NO WAY HE WOULD BE REACTIVATED UNLESS SOMETHING TRULY TERRIFYING WAS GOING ON. DON'T BULLSHIT ME.

I WANT TO KNOW WHAT THAT IS.

IN THE LAST SIX MONTHS, OVER HALF A DOZEN OF THE WORLD'S LEADING VIROLOGISTS AND VIRUS HUNTERS HAVE GONE MISSING.

THE NSA IS LOSING SLEEP, AND WITH GOOD REASON. ONE OR TWO OF THESE PEOPLE IS CAUSE FOR ALARM.

WITH THIS MANY, WE'RE EXPECTING SOMETHING CATASTROPHIC. WE NEED TO AVOID ANOTHER INCIDENT LIKE SHINING LIGHT. HIS PROGRAMMING...

HE'S NOT A MACHINE.

MACHINES HAVE NO SENSE OF LOSS, NO SENSE OF COMPASSION. GREAT SOLDIERS ARE GREAT BECAUSE THEY'RE FIGHTING FOR SOMETHING OTHER THAN *ORDERS*.

EVEN IF YOU DON'T AGREE WITH MY METHODS, I HAVE TO DO THIS MY WAY. I NEED COMPLETE AUTONOMY.

I CAN GIVE YOU THAT FOR SIX TO EIGHT MONTHS AT THE MOST, AMANDA, BUT THERE ARE NO GUARANTEES.

THE ENTIRE PROGRAM IS AT THE MERCY OF THE DOD, AND IF THEY WANT TO DEPLOY HIM, THERE ISN'T A WHOLE HELL OF A LOT I CAN DO.

THEN WE'D BETTER GET STARTED.

I HAVE STARTED HYPE'S ACTIVATION PROTOCOLS. HE'LL BE AWAKE IN A FEW MINUTES.

I THOUGHT WE AGREED TO CALL HIM BY HIS NAME?

FINE. *NOAH* WILL BE AWAKE SOON. I'LL GIVE YOU SPACE TO GET TO KNOW EACH OTHER.

HELLO, AMANDA MARR. IT IS A PLEASURE TO FINALLY MEET YOU.

UH...HELLO, NOAH.

ARE YOU SURE? HE HASN'T MET ME, AND A FAMILIAR FACE WOULD PROBABLY BE A GOOD THING FOR HIM TO SEE.

WE DOWNLOADED YOUR FILE TO HIS SLEEP INTERFACE SO THERE WILL BE NO SURPRISES.

MAY I TOUCH YOUR FACE?

WHAT? I GUESS.

THANK YOU.

SO YOU KNOW WHO I AM?

I DO.

YOU ARE BEHAVIORAL PSYCHOLOGIST AMANDA MARR.

I'M ALSO HERE TO HELP YOU UNDERSTAND WHO YOU ARE AND WHAT YOUR PURPOSE IS BEYOND BEING A SOLDIER.

YOUR SKIN IS VERY SOFT.

PLEASE TRY TO FOCUS.

NOAH, LOOK ME IN THE EYES.

SOCIAL CUES ARE PART OF WHAT MAKES US HUMAN. YOU MIGHT BE HYPER AWARE, BUT YOU'RE ALSO OBLIVIOUS TO SOME OF THE MOST BASIC COMPONENTS OF INTERPERSONAL RELATIONSHIPS.

YOU ARE SAYING I AM LIKE A CHILD.

IN SOME WAYS YOU ARE.

LOOK, FOR THE FIRST FEW WEEKS, I'M GOING TO BE WAKING YOU UP EVERY SINGLE DAY FOR FORTY-FIVE MINUTES. NOT A LONG PERIOD OF TIME.

WE HAVE TO MOVE QUICKLY. I WAS GIVEN ONLY EIGHT MONTHS TO GET YOU MISSION READY.

PUT THIS ON. IT WILL HELP ME FOCUS AND KEEP YOU WARM.

MY BODY CAN ADJUST TO ANY TEMPERATURE. AS LOW AS -89.2 CELSIUS, WHICH WAS RECORDED AT THE VOSTOK STATION IN ANTARCTICA...

JACKET ON. STOP SPOUTING FACTS AT ME.

OKAY, LET'S BEGIN. WHAT IS YOUR EARLIEST MEMORY?

I OPENED MY EYES AND SAW THE SMILING FACES OF MY DOCTORS.

HOW DID THAT MAKE YOU FEEL?

FEEL?

TWO WEEKS LATER.

I JUST GOT WORD WE NEED TO ACCELERATE HIS DEVELOPMENT.

ACCELERATE?

FOUR WEEKS.

THEY'RE GOING TO HAVE TO WAIT.

THEY'RE NOT GOING TO WAIT. THE WORLD CAN'T WAIT.

YOU NAMED HIM NOAH FOR A REASON. THE FLOOD IS COMING, AMANDA. SO YOU'D BETTER HAVE HIM READY.

HE'S STILL RAW. HIS SOCIAL SKILLS ARE AT A FOURTH-GRADE LEVEL.

YOU GET HIM AS FAR AS YOU CAN IN THE TIME ALLOTTED. IF WE HAVE TO, WE CAN SWITCH TO COMBAT MODE.

NO, THAT'S WHAT PUT HIM IN THAT CHAMBER FOR YEARS.

WELL, NEXT WEEK I'M TAKING HIM OUT THEN. IF WE'RE GOING TO GET THIS DONE, I NEED HIM TO EXPERIENCE THE VERY THINGS HE THINKS HE KNOWS SO MUCH ABOUT.

YOU'VE GOT CLEARANCE AND A CREW READY TO TAKE YOU BOTH ANYWHERE YOU LIKE.

AMANDA, I'M NOT BLIND.

JUST FOCUS ON YOUR WORK AND GET THIS DONE.

HE REALLY IS AMAZING, YOU KNOW? THERE IS SO MUCH I CAN SHOW HIM.

I DO... AND I ALSO KNOW HUMAN NATURE.

WHAT ARE YOU SAYING?

ASSHOLE.

THEY REASONED AGAINST THIS, BUT I MADE THE RIGHT ARGUMENT AND HAD THEM BRING US HERE, RIGHT SMACK IN THE MIDDLE OF THE CITY. SURE, IT'S DANGEROUS, BUT OUR ONLY TIME TOGETHER HAS BEEN IN A CONTROLLED ENVIRONMENT.

I NEEDED TO PUSH NOAH HARDER, HAVE HIS SENSES TESTED, AND REALLY SEE WHAT HE COULD DO IN THE REAL WORLD.

WHY ARE WE HERE? IS THERE A DANGER?

NO. I WANTED TO GET YOU OUT OF THE FACILITY.

WHY?

YOU ONLY HAVE FORTY-FIVE MINUTES A DAY TO EXPERIENCE THE WORLD, NOAH.

THERE'S MORE TO LIFE THAN YOU CAN POSSIBLY IMAGINE, AND I THINK LEARNING THIS WILL HELP YOUR TRAINING.

OPEN YOURSELF TO THE PARK. STOP AND USE ALL YOUR SENSES.

TELL ME... WHAT DO YOU FEEL? WHAT DO YOU SEE, HEAR, AND TASTE?

A SMILE TURNED TO A LAUGH AND THEN BACK TO A GRIN. HIS HEAD TILTED AS IF CAPTURING A BEAT IN THE DISTANCE, AND HIS BODY SWAYED, BECOMING ONE WITH IT. HIS CHIN LIFTED AS HE TOOK A BREATH, CAPTURING A MOMENTARY SCENT, IF ONLY FOR A SECOND.

WATCHING HIM TAKE ALL THIS IN, I WANTED NOTHING MORE THAN TO TAKE HIM AWAY AND SHOW HIM THE WORLD HE MIGHT NEVER GET TO SEE.

THEN, IT HAPPENED...

NOT NOW...

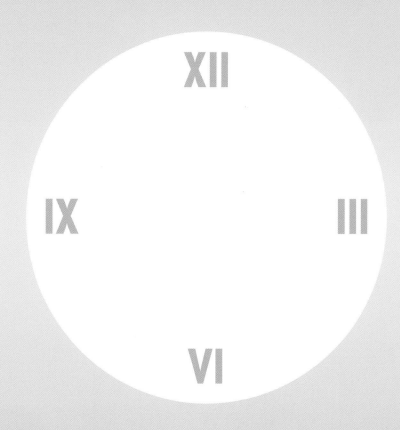

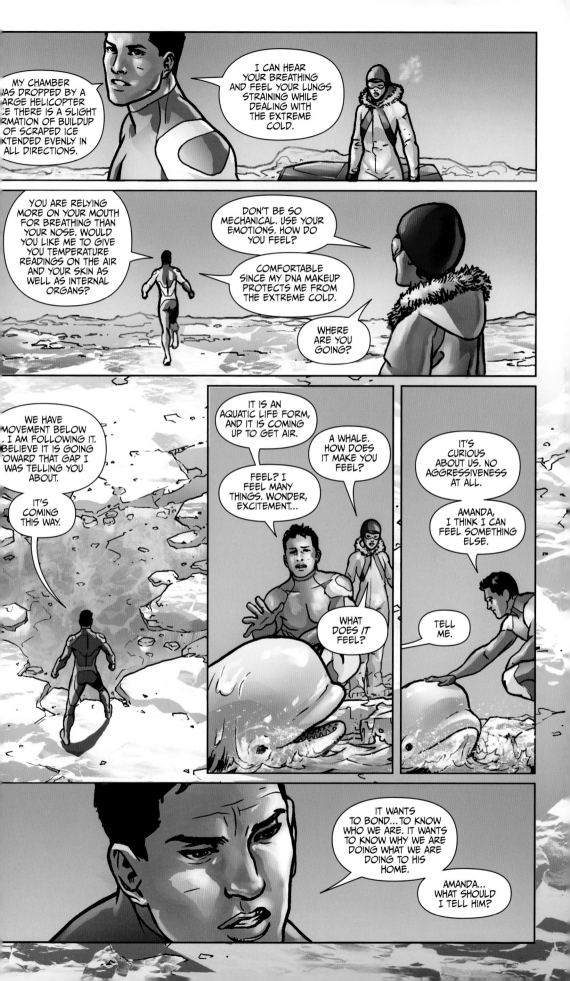

YOU'VE GOT THREE MINUTES LEFT, NOAH. I'VE GOT TO GET YOU BACK. SAY GOOD-BYE, AND LET'S MAKE OUR WAY TO THE CHAMBER. I DON'T THINK I CAN CARRY YOU THAT FAR.

HANG ON. TRUST ME.

I DO, BUT...

RELAX YOUR BREATHING. I CAN FEEL YOUR PULSE QUICKENING.

HE LIFTS ME AS IF I WEIGH NOTHING. I CAN FEEL HIS WARM BREATH ON MY FACE.

HIS HARD, MUSCULAR BODY IS GIVING OFF HEAT.

I HAVEN'T BEEN CARRIED SINCE I WAS A CHILD.

NOAH, YOU REALLY COMMUNICATED WITH THAT WHALE, DIDN'T YOU?

YES. HE ASKED IF YOU WERE MY MATE.

WHAT DID YOU TELL HIM?

IT IS A SECRET. TIME IS...

WAIT, SECRETS? SINCE WHEN...?

WELL I'LL BE.

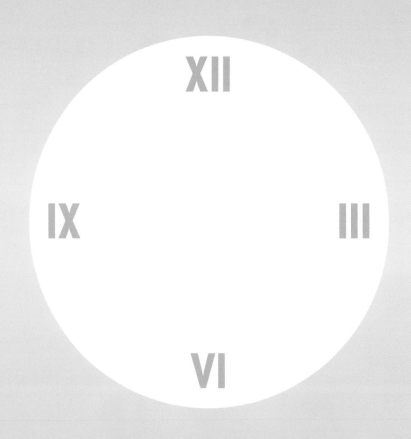

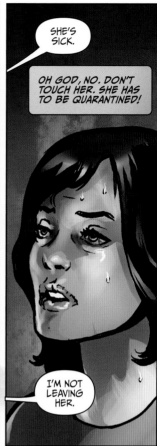

REDGRAVE, CAN YOU HEAR ME?

I HEAR YOU, NOAH. GOOD WORK.

NO, NOT GOOD. YOU SENT AMANDA TO MEET THE MISSING DOCTOR...

SIR, YOUR LEVELS ARE SPIKING...!

NOT YET!

REDGRAVE, WHY DID OKAFOR CONTACT AMANDA AND SAY SHE'D ONLY SPEAK TO HER? DID THEY KNOW EACH OTHER?

NO. SOMEONE INSIDE THE PROGRAM BETRAYED US. THEY SET UP THE MEET AND GAVE OKAFOR AMANDA'S NAME. WE'RE WORKING ON FINDING THE PERSON, BUT TODAY AMANDA IS SAFE THANKS TO YOU.

THEY TRIED TO HURT HER BECAUSE OF ME?

WELCOME TO THE WORLD OF GROWNUPS, NOAH. IT ISN'T PRETTY, BUT THAT'S WHY WE NEED YOU.

GET SOME REST AND DON'T WORRY ABOUT AMANDA. WE'LL DO EVERYTHING WE CAN FOR HER.

Alternate cover by
DAVE JOHNSON

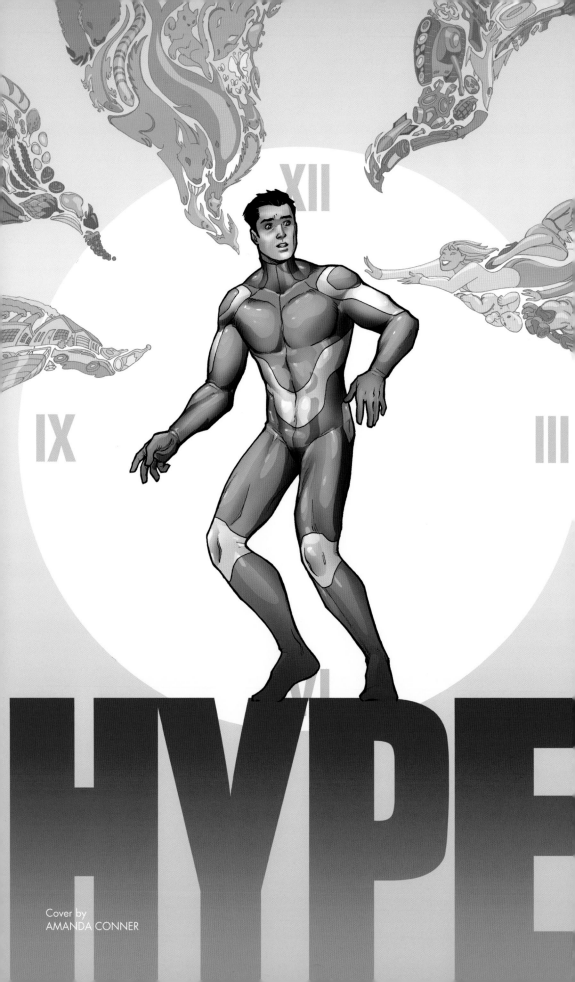

XII

IX

III

HYPE

JIMMY PALMIOTTI

Jimmy Palmiotti is a multi-award-winning writer and comic artist and the co-founder of Event Comics, Black Bull Media, Marvel Knights, and, most recently PaperFilms, where he currently partners with Amanda Conner and Justin Gray. Together they have created and co-created *Monolith, 21 Down, The Resistance,* and *The Twilight Experiment* for DC Comics as well as *The New West, The Pro, Gatecrasher, Beautiful Killer, Ash, Cloudburst, Trigger Girl 6, Splatterman, Trailblazer, Retrovirus, The Last Resort, Delete, Sex and Violence, Forager,* and *Painkiller Jane,* which was turned into a SyFy original TV series starring Kristanna Loken and recently optioned for the movie screen.

Jimmy has partnered with several clients, such as Nike, Disney, Warner Brothers, Lion's Gate, Fox, New Line, 2KGames, and THQ games. He has co-written, with Justin Gray, on the video game *Injustice: Gods Among Us* for NeatherRealm Studios and *DCU vs. Mortal Kombat.* At Marvel, Jimmy teamed with Joe Quesada to create the Marvel Knights imprint and usher in a radical change at Marvel Comics still felt to this day. He and Justin Gray were tapped to adapt the award-winning novel *Wool* for an Amazon exclusive digital graphic novel series.

JUSTIN GRAY

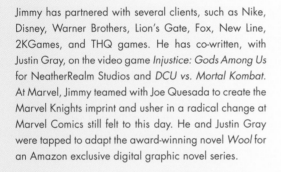

Over the last decade, Justin Gray has worked on comic book titles that include *Power Girl, Harley Quinn and PowerGirl, 21 Down, Jonah Hex, Marvel Adventures, The Monolith, Daughters of the Dragon, Tattered Man, Abbadon, Delete, Trancers, Lone Ranger,* and *Wool* for Amazon Jet City Comics.

He's also written for children's magazines, film, television, and video games. Prior to his work as a professional author, Justin was a fossil hunter, advocate for victims of crime, and a microphotographer capturing rare images of 20-million-year-old insects trapped in amber.

JAVIER PINA

Javier Pino is a Spanish artist who began his career in the mid-1990s, drawing for the *451º* fanzine. For Semic France, he is an illustrator of the series *Strangers,* alternating with fellow Spanish artists like Manuel Garcia and Fernando Blanco. Pino has worked on *Manhunter, Swamp Thing, Birds of Prey, Detective Comics, Resurrection Man,* and *Superman* for DC Comics, as well as *Solider Zero* for BOOM Comics.

ALESSIA NOCERA

Alessia Nocera is the chief colorist for GG Studios and works for Scuola Internazionale di Comics in Italy. Her past collaborations have included works for Disney and Marvel. Her beautiful coloring can also be found for work by Zenescope Entertainment, several GG Studio titles (*The One, Mediterranea, Extinction Seed, Gore*), the historical graphic novel *Napoleon* for Glenat, and other publishers. At Scuola Internazionale di Comics at the Neapolitan branch, she teaches Digital Coloring and Illustration.

BILL TORTOLINI

An accomplished art director and graphic designer, Bill began designing and lettering in the comic industry more than a decade ago and has worked with many of comics' top creators and publishers, including Marvel, IDW, Image, Kickstart, Disney, MTV, and Del Rey.

Bill is an avid Bruins, Patriots, and Red Sox fan (and hopes Jimmy does not hold that against him). Bill lives in Massachusetts, with his wife, three children, and his sometimes loyal dog, Oliver.

JOHN J. HILL

John J. Hill is a freelance creative director and designer working in comics, technology, advertising, gaming, and entertainment. He has developed and designed campaigns, branding, packaging, coffee table books, and other creative for Adobe, Aeropostale, Atlantic Records, Disney, Feral Audio, GM, Midnight Oil, NHL, Random House, Zynga, and many more. In the comics industry, John has worked on hundreds of properties creating logos, designing graphic novels, illustrating covers, and lettering. Current projects include lettering *SuperZero* for AfterShock and *Nailbiter* for Image, designing books for Disney Press and Legendary, and a vertigo-inducing amount of others.

"WHAT IS THE SILENCE OF SIX, AND WHAT ARE YOU GOING TO DO ABOUT IT?"

These are the last words uttered by 17-year-old Max Stein's best friend, Evan, just moments before he kills himself after hacking into the live-streaming presidential debate at their high school.

Haunted by the unforgettable image of Evan's death, Max's entire world is upended as he suddenly finds himself the target of a corporate-government witch hunt. Fearing for his life and fighting for his own innocence, Max goes on the run with no one to trust and too many unanswered questions.

Max must dust off his own hacking skills and maneuver through the dangerous labyrinth of underground hacktivist networks, ever-shifting alliances and virtual identities—all the while hoping to find the truth behind the "Silence of Six" before it's too late.

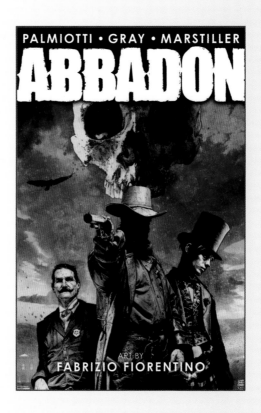

FROM PROLIFIC WRITERS Jimmy Palmiotti & Justin Gray (*Jonah Hex, Power Girl, 21 Down*) with art by Fabrizio Fiorentino & Alessia Nocera, *Abbadon* tells the tale of a city steeped in sin. The western boomtown of Abbadon is poised for a bright future until it experiences a series of gruesome murders. U.S. Marshal Wes Garrett is called to town to solve them.

A legendary lawman, Garrett is known for having trapped and killed a notorious murderer named "Bloody Bill" who once cut a brutal swath across the country and left scores of mutilated men, women, and children in his wake. Now Garrett's arrival in Abbadon has revealed a secret that Sheriff Colt Dixon has desperately been trying to conceal: the recent murders have all echoed the style of the killer Garrett supposedly stopped years ago. Garrett and Dixon join forces to uncover the killer's identity in a town so full of corruption that everyone is a suspect.